MW00627509

FINANCIALLY
SPEAKING

How to Deliver High-Impact
Presentations for the
Financial Services Industry

ROBERT A. LEO

Compliments of
MFS Fund Distributors
800-343-2829 (press 1)

Copyright © 2004 by Robert A. Leo.
All rights reserved.
Printed in the United States of America.
Library of Congress Control Number: 2003115252
ISBN: 0-9747868-0-2
Book design by Sarah Isaacs, *North Fork Press*

Dedication

For my parents Ernest and Mildred,
who gave me everything.

To Dorothy,
for your love and patience.

To Michael, Jaymeson, Cameron and Brody,
Kathy, Steven, Katelyn and Grant,
for the pride and pure joy you give me.

· ACKNOWLEDGEMENTS ·

You cannot have a successful 35-year career in the financial services industry without guidance and support from many people. I am deeply indebted to the following people:

Bill Leakas hired me as a retail broker at Hayden Stone's Dayton, Ohio office in 1969 and served as a role model my first years in the business. His friendship and support has meant much to me. Bill is a Financial Advisor at Smith Barney and a true professional in every sense of the word.

Mike Panitch gave me my first opportunity to manage that same Dayton, Ohio branch. I learned much from Mike over the years. When he first hired me, he told me, "Surround yourself with great people." I took it to heart and it made all the difference.

Joe Plumeri brought me into corporate headquarters at Shearson Lehman American Express as Director of Sales. For five years I worked closely with Joe and learned more about marketing, sales and strategic planning than in the previous 15 years. In 1989 he asked me to run the mutual fund department, an equally fortuitous opportunity. Joe is Chairman and CEO of Willis Group Holdings.

In 1994 Bill Scott hired me as Director of the Broker Dealer channel at MFS Fund Distributors. Bill served as my mentor and friend for the next ten years. Bill, an outstanding manager and strategic thinker, continues to serve MFS as Vice Chairman.

For the preparation of this book, I want to thank and gratefully acknowledge Karen Murray for her editing, as well as her guidance and encouragement.

My thanks also to Cindy Brouillette, not only for her typing and retyping, but for her generous support and positive attitude the ten years I was at MFS Fund Distributors.

· TABLE OF CONTENTS ·

· FOREWORD ·

This delightful little book by Bob Leo documents a wonderfully liberating truth: that before public speaking is an art – and even if it never achieves that level – it is a practical craft. With forethought, purpose and practice, anyone can become a very good speaker by following Bob's simple but compelling plan.

Being himself a leader rather than a manager, Bob's essential perception is that speaking to a group is fundamentally an act of leadership. He therefore holds that you not only don't ever have to make a mediocre speech *but that you don't have the right to do so.* Educating and motivating others by speaking effectively to them becomes, in this view, a kind of moral obligation. And as speakers we can always discharge that obligation, with Bob's guidance.

This is a book of immense practical wisdom, consummate professionalism, utter lack of pretension and great personal charm – exactly like its author. Antoine de Saint-Exupéry said that perfection is achieved not when there is nothing more to add, but when there is nothing left to take away. In distilling the craft of effective speaking down to its pure essence, Bob has, in my judgment, achieved something very close to that ideal of perfection. And reading *Financially Speaking* has already made me a better speaker.

Nick Murray

· INTRODUCTION ·

Of all the talents bestowed upon men, none is more precious as the gift of oratory. He who enjoys it wields a power more durable than that of a great king. He is an independent force in the world.

– Winston Churchill

While it is doubtful that any of us will ever be called on to help save our nation and its people, we do have the ability to make a difference, not only in our own lives and careers, but also in the lives and careers of others. Whether you're a retail advisor, branch manager or president of a financial services organization, you have the ability to lead and motivate through public speaking. The truth is, if you're a manager in our industry, you have that obligation. And, of course, the more skillful you are as a speaker, the more rewarding the experience – financially and emotionally.

Great speakers are not born with that ability, but develop it through study, practice and experience. *Financially Speaking* will give you all the tools and information you need to make strong, impactful presentations. It will provide:

• An analysis of key issues involved in understanding your audience and the topics that they will find most compelling.

• A roadmap for structuring your presentation to get the audience's attention and keep it.

• Hundreds of quotes, anecdotes and stories that add interest and credibility to you and to your presentation.

Getting in front of a group to speak is really about leadership. It's about having a point of view, and convincing people that your point of view is the right one. It's about proposing solutions to issues and moving people in a direction to address those issues. By following the concepts and ideas outlined in *Financially Speaking,* you will not only become a better speaker, but ultimately a better leader.

PART ONE

■

Getting Ready

■ 1. KNOW YOUR AUDIENCE

A few years ago I watched an institutional salesperson give a presentation to a group of retail investors. It wasn't a pretty sight. He was so used to speaking to sophisticated investors that his delivery and content went right over the investors' heads. Bottom line – no sales.

Before preparing your presentation, give serious thought to doing some of the following:

- Find out what type of program has been planned. Who else is speaking? How much time do you have? Does the event have a specific theme or purpose?

- Profile the typical person in the audience – age, education, knowledge of your topic, income, etc.

- Interview audience members or those in charge of the meeting to discuss the topic and any ideas they have about your presentation.

- Ask yourself what the audience's reaction to your presentation might be. Clearly, speaking to a group of total strangers offers a different set of challenges than does speaking to a group of people you know well. Think about the tone of the presentation and the types of persuasive techniques you will be using.

- Put yourself in the audience's place. I use this idea a lot not only in speaking situations, but also in putting together marketing and sales campaigns. Literally try to imagine you're in the audience! What's their frame of reference or background concerning the topic? Why should they care? What will move them to listen and act?

Always remember that the presentation *is not about you.* It's about the audience. The more you know about them and their circumstances, the better you can relate to them, and make them feel comfortable about who you are and what you're saying. And, in the end, your presentation will be more effective.

To quote Edward H. McCarthy in his book *Speechwriting,* "If there is an anvil on which the metal of the speech is shaped and tested, it is the audience." Quite simply, you can't know too much about your audience and the speaking situation.

■ 2. DEVELOP YOUR THEME & OBJECTIVE

I love the exchange in *Alice in Wonderland* where Alice asks, "Would you tell me please, which way I ought to walk from here?" The Cheshire cat's reply, "That depends a good deal on where you want to get to."

Great presentations start with a laser-sharp theme and objective. I remember reading this many years ago, and I've seen it repeated in many books – *reduce your theme and objective to just a few sentences.* This will guide the subsequent growth of the speech and help you make the right choices concerning supporting research, information and discussion points.

Here are some examples:

Theme – Asset allocation is an investor's most important tool.

Objective – Convince seminar participants to work with me in establishing a proper asset allocation for their investment portfolio.

◆ ◆ ◆ ◆

Theme – One of the best ways to insure strong, ongoing revenue is through establishing 401(k) business. MFS offers multiple product solutions and great service.

Objective – I want advisors to get active in 401(k) business and use MFS as their solution provider.

◆ ◆ ◆ ◆

Theme – Value-added programs allow you to help branch managers and their advisors be more successful. By helping them be more successful, they will help you be more successful.

Objective – Motivate our field force to learn and implement our value-added programs.

To develop a well-defined theme and objective, begin by asking yourself some questions.

1. What occasion has brought me in front of this audience?

2. What are the expectations of the audience, if any? What's on their minds?

3. What are my superiors expecting from my presentation?

4. What are the key issues facing the industry and, more specifically, the group I'm speaking to?

5. What is the purpose of my presentation?
   - To inform?
   - To teach?
   - To persuade and perhaps motivate?
   - To entertain (except on that rare occasion, it should always do that)?

6. What effect should my presentation have on the audience?
   - Change their opinion?
   - Convince them to take some action?
   - Impart knowledge to them?

You ask these questions so you can clearly identify the need of the audience. If you get it right, it's much more likely that your presentation will hold their interest and, most importantly, address their issues and concerns.

In 1990, shortly after I had taken over the Mutual Fund Department at Shearson Lehman Brothers, I was asked to be on a panel at the Investment Company Institute's annual meeting. I was joined by Vanguard's Jack Bogle and a bank CEO. Each of us was to discuss distribution from our side of the business. I represented the B/D perspective. Frankly, being new to the mutual fund industry, I was a little nervous and not quite sure of what to say. For a month I worked on my presentation, which contained lots of statistics and was quite dry. I wasn't happy with it.

About two weeks before the presentation, it suddenly struck me – what the vast majority of the audience wants to know is how they can create more sales within the broker/dealer channel. So, why don't I give them what they want? I totally rebuilt my presentation with a new theme: Broker-distributed funds will be the fastest growing channel in our industry and here's how you can participate in that growth. I was very pleased with the new presentation and received strong, positive feedback after the meeting.

I fulfilled the obligation of the panel, but I did it in a way that was of interest to the audience and of *value* to them. Maybe that's the ultimate question you must ask yourself as you develop your theme and objective. *Will your audience walk away from your presentation feeling that it was of real value?* If so, you're on your way to building a great presentation.

■ 3. OUTLINE AND ORGANIZE

So far you've analyzed the audience and established your theme and objective. Perhaps you have some idea of what you want to say, but haven't really organized it. Writing an outline is the first step in constructing a successful speech. The opening and closing of your speech follow naturally.

Let's go through the preparation of an outline. To do that, I would like you to consider an imaginary situation based on a potentially real incident and speech. You're a top sales executive at a money management organization or brokerage firm, and you've been asked to speak to a group of senior retail advisors. With the current environment what it is, they have asked you to speak on the topic of *Building Trust with Clients*. All they have provided you with is a recent survey from the Securities Industry Association that shows that *trustworthy* is the number one characteristic that investors want from their investment advisor.

Research

The first question that comes to mind when you hear the topic is, "Do I know enough about it to make a great presentation?" For the record, I have turned down speaking opportunities because I felt I could not speak with confidence on the topic and did not have time to do the research. You should too! As a wise man once said, "Better not to speak and let people think you don't know, than to speak and give them proof."

In this particular case, you do have some strong ideas on the topic, but realize you will need more information to do a proper job. To conduct research, first see if anyone has written any books or articles on the topic. You might want to interview some experts (successful advisors) to get their opinion. And, of course, the Internet has virtually unlimited information on many topics. Remember, as you do your research, you're looking for everything and anything that will not only support your topic, but also add color and life to it – quotations, statistics, anecdotes, humor, etc. Normally, this part of the presentation, known as the *body* of the speech, consists of three to four major points with sub-points underneath them.

Make a List

After you've given thought to the topic and done some research, list the points you want to make. For the speech on *Trust*, here is a list of 13 points:

1. Trust is the heart and essence of what our business is all about.
2. It is the number one characteristic investors want from an advisor.
3. Investors want to understand how their money will be invested.
4. Needs-based selling is critical to building trust.
5. Investors must have realistic expectations. If they expect too much, they will be disappointed.
6. Never sell product on the first interview.
7. Ongoing communication will be a key part of keeping the client's trust.
8. Listening skills are critical.
9. References could be a great way to help prospects establish trust.
10. Many successful advisors conduct regular seminars for clients.
11. Asking great questions helps prospects/clients have confidence and trust in you.
12. An annual survey would be a great test of client satisfaction.
13. Conduct an annual review of your clients' holdings in person.

Organize

There are a number of ways to organize the body of your speech. It could be as simple as making sure your strongest points are first and last (the audience is more likely to remember them), or it could be more structured.

For instance, you could organize your speech in chronological order – that is based on a sequence of events taking place. You could organize your speech in topical order, dividing the subject matter into a smaller set of "topics." If you had to explain a very complicated issue or process, you might want to use a simple-to-complex order to do so. The point is to consider dividing your topic into a number of smaller categories in order for the audience to more easily comprehend and absorb the information.

Regarding the *Trust* presentation, as I review the key points, they seem to fall under three major topics. When you organize the list, it might look like this:

I.   Getting Ready
- Do you have a disciplined approach to investing, and is it in writing for your clients?
- You should establish a list of referrals.
- Are you selling using a consultative approach?
- Do you have a series of questions to establish the needs of the client?

II. The Initial Interview
- Stop talking so much and listen.
- Manage the client's expectations.
- Avoid selling during the initial interview – set up the next appointment to review recommendations.

III. Maintaining Trust
- Ongoing communication is key – set up a system to stay in touch.
- Do an annual review in person.
- Send out a satisfaction survey yearly.

Of course, this is just a bare bones outline, but it does put your presentation in a format which makes it easier to explain and comprehend. In the next section of the book, we'll discuss how to present this type of information in an interesting and dynamic way.

PART TWO

■

The Speech

■ 4. GREAT BEGINNINGS

Richard Dowis, in his excellent book *The Lost Art of the Great Speech,* writes, "Although a good opening does not guarantee a good speech, a bad opening almost always guarantees a bad speech."

That happened to me in 1986 when I was National Sales Manager at Shearson American Express. I had just taken over the responsibility for the Branch Fixed Income Coordinators. They were retail advisors who worked with their branch managers to support the corporate, government and municipal bond business. I was to be the after-dinner speaker to 125 coordinators. As I listened to the other speakers and attendees during the day, they referred to retail advisors as "brokers." At the corporate level, we were trying to change the image of the retail "broker." Part of that change was an announcement a few months earlier that they would be called "financial consultants."

When I got up to speak, my introductory remarks were about how important it was that we position ourselves correctly in the industry, how we all should embrace this new term "financial consultant," etc. I didn't mean to, but in fact, I lectured the group. And in doing so, I dug myself into a hole I couldn't get out of. Based on the hostile Q&A that followed, as well as the feedback I received, it would probably score as the worst presentation I ever gave. The only upside was that I learned a valuable lesson – the beginning of a presentation is crucial!

At a minimum, your opening comments should:

1. Capture the audience's attention.

2. Establish your credibility.

3. Create a bond of good will with the audience.

4. Reveal the topic or theme of the speech, as well as your viewpoint.

This may seem like a lot, but with some thought and planning, it can and should be done in three to four minutes. Let's review each part.

Capture the Audience's Attention

I read a book that declared you only have eight seconds to get an audience's attention. I can't say how the author came up with that exact number, but he's correct in saying you don't have a lot of time. People in our business have a lot going on in their lives and a lot on their minds. They can be distracted easily. On top of that, it's likely that the audience has not assembled just to hear you speak. You may be part of a day-long agenda. Have you ever spoken at a branch breakfast or lunch meeting? Did they come to hear you or to eat a free meal? YOUR OPENING COMMENTS MUST GRAB THEIR ATTENTION! And please don't start your presentation with a lot of pleasantries or meandering comments. Everyone does. Be different. After your introduction, a simple "thank you" is fine.

Here are some great ways to start.

1. The Dramatic Statement

- Today the mutual fund industry has over $2 trillion in money market funds earning 0.5%. Investors have long-term goals with short-term investments. Something's wrong!

- Four out of five advisors in this room can double their income within five years.

  The dramatic statement should be unusual, novel or unexpected, and should always create some tension. It should wake the audience up and let them know that you have something important to say. It also has the advantage of introducing your topic right up front, and allows you to transition into the body of your speech more easily.

2. Ask a Question – Direct or Rhetorical

- Have you ever worked with a client for a number of years, thought everything was great, and all of a sudden received instructions to transfer the account to another Broker/Dealer?

- How much of a portfolio's performance is attributed to asset allocation versus stock selection and market timing?

Asking questions can be a powerful opening. When the question is asked, it begs for an answer. It gains the audience's attention immediately.

A few years ago, I conducted workshops for advisors on how to build and retain trust with their clients. I started out by holding up a $20 bill and asking, "I'm willing to exchange this $20 for $10. Who's interested?" No one raised their hand immediately. Then a few hands went up. I exchanged the $20 for the $10 with the first person who raised their hand, and then I asked another question. "Why didn't the rest of you raise your hand?" They responded that they didn't trust me; they thought there was a "catch." And, of course, this led perfectly into my subject matter. It's one of my favorite openings, even though it costs me $10 to do it.

3. Humor

I love humor as an opening. It can get the audience's attention and create some good will at the same time. But you must be careful. The humor must have some context and relation to what's happening – your introduction, the location, the audience, the occasion, etc. In other words, *this is not the time for a joke*.

Part Three of this book provides a number of humorous openings.

Here are a few:

- If you have a tough spot on the program –

  I feel like we're in a javelin-throwing contest. I've lost the coin toss, and I'm receiving.

- Maybe there is a smaller-than-expected turnout –

  I recently spoke at a meeting where there was only one person in the audience. I figured "Hey, the show must go on," so I did my 30-minute presentation. I finished, and was about to leave, when the guy in the audience got all excited and said, "You can't leave." I asked him why not. He said, "Because I'm the next speaker."

In 1990, when I was at Shearson Lehman Brothers, I was scheduled to speak late in the day at an industry conference. Shearson had been struggling with a recent merger, and a few of the analysts before me had some really negative comments about the firm. When I was introduced, and the name Shearson Lehman Brothers was mentioned, you could feel the audience stiffen up. I went up to the lectern, slowly looked out at the audience and said, "Yes, Shearson Lehman Brothers. There are still some of us around." It got a good laugh and some applause. You're not looking to have them rolling in the aisles (although go for it if you can), you're just trying to get a chuckle and relax everyone.

One other caveat. There are humorous stories I told a few years ago that in this politically correct environment I wouldn't touch. If you have any doubt about the suitability of your comments or your ability to use humor in general, don't try it. There are too many other great ways to start a speech.

4. Tell a Story or Anecdote

Storytelling has universal appeal. Before man could write, stories were told to teach and pass history from one generation to another. Today we have multi-billion dollar industries established around storytelling. Everybody loves a good story.

Stories humanize your speech because a story has characters. Stories activate and bring your speech to life because they have a plot (starts, rises, climaxes and closes). And, of course, a story can bring focus and credibility to your speech if it's relevant to your theme. For these reasons, stories can be used effectively for an opening, within the body of your speech and at the end. Don't be afraid to use a few stories with your presentation.

A story can take many forms:

A. The personal incident is perhaps the most powerful because it will be easy for people to relate to and you'll tell it with great conviction.

I remember in the mid-'80s shopping for a high-end amplifier for my stereo system. I got the same treatment at the first three stores I went into. After I stated my interest, the salesperson took me back to the equipment room. Immediately he started telling me about and selling me on the virtues of certain brands and models, getting into esoteric minutiae that I didn't understand and did not have interest in. Result – no sale. The fourth store I went into, something totally different happened. After I explained what I wanted, the salesperson asked, "Mr. Leo, when you listen to your stereo now, what don't you like?" After I answered, he had some other questions. "What type of music do you listen to?" "What type of stereo equipment do you currently have?" "How big is the room you'll be listening in?" All good questions that showed me he cared about me and my needs. Of course, this salesperson took a consultative approach to selling and it worked. Not only did I buy an amplifier, but I also gave him some referrals. It's a wonderful story and one I tell whenever I talk to salespeople about how they should be dealing with their clients.

B. The third-person incident is a story that didn't happen to you, but to someone you know – or it could be something you saw on TV or read about in the newspaper.

In a speech on teamwork, or even if you're just making a point about teamwork, there is a great story about Stacey King during his rookie year with the Chicago Bulls. During one game he scored one point and Michael Jordan scored 69. When a reporter asked King for his reaction to the game, King said, "I'll always remember this as the night that Michael Jordan and I teamed up to score 70 points." Of course, you could then go on to make any number of comments about teamwork, the group you're speaking to, etc.

C. The fictional story is made up for the purpose of your speech. It could be totally fictional, or you could use a scene from a movie, book, TV show, etc.

When I talk to marketing and salespeople about the importance of listening, I love to relate the scene from the Woody Allen movie *Play It Again, Sam*. Woody is on the make in the Museum of Modern Art. He approaches this very attractive young lady who is looking at a rather bizarre contemporary painting. He asks her, "What does that say to you?" She tells him, "It tells me about the utter devastation of all mankind. That we will soon come to a fiery and burning end." In response, Woody asks, "So what are you doing Saturday night?" She tells him, "I'm going to commit suicide." His next question, "So, what about Friday night?" Of course, you then go on to make the point that Woody wasn't listening!

One of the keys to telling a good fictional or humorous story is telling it as though it is totally true. If you feel uncomfortable about that, you can do as I sometimes do at the end and say, "By the way, that was a true story I just made up. But it does illustrate the point..."

You may now be asking yourself, "How will I come up with all these stories when I need them?" There are two answers. First of all, there are hundreds of books published that contain stories, quotes, anecdotes, etc. I've provided a list of my favorites in Part Three of this book. The other way, harder, but in my mind preferred, is to keep track of what you see, hear and experience. If you were to see my Franklin Planner today, it contains 50 pages of "stuff" that happened to me, things I read about or heard. I use it as a resource, particularly if I have only a short time to prepare a speech or presentation. Of course, it is backed up by my home library.

Establish Your Credibility

Clearly your job of speaking is easier if the audience believes that you have knowledge and experience on the subject matter. This will come out (or not) as you make your presentation. But, if you can establish that credibility early, the audience will more readily accept your ideas and proposals.

A few thoughts:

- Speaker bios are often provided to the audience. If so, make sure yours is included.

- A good introduction is essential! Be sure to speak to the person who will introduce you. Ask them if they need help with the introduction. Be prepared to write one out, or better still, come to the meeting with one. And don't feel strange about that. As someone who has introduced hundreds of speakers, I'm always delighted if I can help someone by giving them a proper introduction. I remember in particular a very prominent speaker in our industry who insisted you read his introduction verbatim. Why? So he could then use it to make some jokes about himself and relax the audience.

- When all else fails, you must be prepared to establish your credibility within your opening comments. This can be as simple as mentioning your background. "I've been in the industry for 35 years, and I must admit, it's never been as challenging as the last three or four years." Or, "I've been in the business for 35 years, 15 of those years as a retail advisor and branch manager. I know what it feels like to be on the firing line."

Create a Bond of Good Will

The goal of establishing a positive relationship between yourself and the audience has a variety of names attached to it: good will bond, one-to-one connection, speaker/listener rapport. Whichever term you use, the point is that you're trying to connect with the audience and to induce a feeling of similarity between you and them. You want the audience to feel comfortable with you as a person. The more comfortable they are, the more willing they will be to accept you and your presentation.

Here are some ideas on how to accomplish that:

- We already spoke about humor. Getting an audience to laugh together certainly relaxes the group and can create that good will you're looking for.

- Try to personalize your opening comments to the group or use one of your best stories early in your presentation. It humanizes you and your presentation.

- Always be yourself. After I'd been a retail advisor for six years at Shearson Hayden Stone's Dayton, Ohio office, Mike Panitch, the regional director and an outstanding manager, asked me to become the branch manager in the same office. I wanted the job badly, but was concerned about running the branch after being an advisor there.

I asked Mike how I should interact with the office. Mike said, "Be yourself. It got you this far." It was great advice. That same advice applies to speechmaking – be yourself. If you are liked and respected away from the podium, you probably will be when you're *at* the podium.

- In your opening comments, point out similarities between you and the audience. This could be your background, work, beliefs, any shared experiences. Just be sure you don't force something that doesn't exist.

Reveal the Topic or Theme

At this point, you've gained the audience's attention and started to connect with them. You may have already used your introduction to reveal your topic. If not, now is the time. Remember that your audience's patience, particularly at this point, is limited. They want to know your topic *and its value to them.*

Listening is an active process, so you're trying to motivate the audience to listen, and give them an indication of what to expect. This should be done in a clear and direct manner.

Here are some examples:

- Every study in the last 40 years has shown that asset allocation is, by far, the most important factor in the performance of an investment portfolio. Tonight we'll talk about asset allocation and how you can build your portfolio to maximize potential returns and reduce volatility.

- The Securities Industry Association conducted a study with investors showing that *trust* was the most important factor to them in dealing with an advisor. I want to talk to you about the best ways to establish and retain trust with your clients.

- The year 2004 is a critical one to our firm's financial well-being. It's also a year where your performance on the job is very important. With that in mind, I want to share with you our business plans for the coming year and elicit your feedback and ideas.

▪ 5. MAKING YOUR POINT

Now let's address the *body* of the presentation. Whether your objective is to inform the audience or motivate them to take some action, this is where you present and develop your ideas. We've already discussed some powerful speaking techniques that can be used during the opening. ALL OF THEM, PARTICULARLY STORYTELLING AND HUMOR, CAN AND SHOULD BE USED IN THE BODY OF YOUR PRESEN-TATION. Here are three additional techniques that can be used.

Statistics

Our industry is built on numbers and statistics. Whether it's the size of the High Net Worth Market, the three-year annualized return of a mutual fund, or the earnings growth of your own company, statistics can be a powerful resource within your presentation. Statistics are especially useful when you want to make your point seem more precise or more impressive. Just be sure to use them sparingly. Don't bore your audience with endless numbers.

Here are just a few ways to use statistics:

1. Absolute Magnitude

There are over seven trillion dollars in the mutual fund industry. To give you a sense of how much that is, let me point out the difference between a million and a trillion. A million seconds is $12\frac{1}{2}$ days; a trillion seconds is 36,000 years.

2. Quantitative Comparison

Mr. and Mrs. Smith, the cumulative return of the S&P 500 over the last five years has been 15.2%, while your domestic portfolio is up 32.6%.

3. Statistical Trends

Separately Managed Accounts has a 15% per year growth rate over the past five years. It is the fastest growing segment of our industry.

4. Suggest Relationships

We've added ten percent to our sales force, but our sales are only up two percent.

<u>Quotations</u>

Quotations can add credibility, emphasis and authority to your presentation. Imagine having Peter Drucker on the platform with you when you talk about management. How about Peter Lynch or Warren Buffett when you speak about investing? Quotations allow you to bring into your presentation the wisdom of the ages! Once again, as with all speech techniques and devices, don't overdo it, but quotations can fit beautifully into the opening, body or close of your presentation.

There are several ways to use quotations:

1. Quote an expert to support your point.

   It's difficult to change, but it's critical we change with the times. As Tom Peters pointed out, "Today, loving change, tumult, even chaos is a prerequisite for survival, let alone success."

2. Quote someone who has creatively captured your theme or a certain aspect of your speech.

   Today most investors remain cautious, and many are frightened of investing. It was Ralph Waldo Emerson who said, "Knowledge is the antidote to fear." I want to talk to you about how our industry can better educate investors.

3. The indirect quote doesn't use the exact words of the quote; rather, it paraphrases. It may be preferred because it allows you to shorten the quote while still getting your point across.

   When I think about excellence, I think about what Maurice Greene, the current world recordholder in the 100 meters, said when reporters asked him how it feels to be the fastest person in the world. He basically said that if I think about being #1, I'll be beat. To be #1,

I've got to train like I'm #2.

Some final thoughts on using quotations:

- Keep them short. Once, during a speech on *Change*, I quoted a stanza from Bob Dylan's *All Along the Watchtower*. The audience was lost.

- Make sure they're not too familiar or trite.

- Give credit where credit is due.

- Never say, "Quote, unquote." Use the tone of your voice or a pause to let the audience know where the quote begins and ends.

Analogies

Analogies not only add color to your presentation, but also bring into sharp focus the point you're trying to make. Additionally, they can be helpful in explaining something that may be difficult for the audience to understand.

- The best golfer is not the one who hits the most great shots, but the one who hits the fewest bad ones – just like with investing.

- When is the best time to buy? I call it the Diaper Indicator. The best time to buy is when investors are wetting their pants.

- Time is like the Archimedes lever in investing.
  – Charles Ellis

Some additional notes concerning the body of your presentation and making your point:

- **Don't waste time – get to your core theme.**

- **Be sure to replay and remind the audience of the central theme.**

- **Follow a logical order.**

- **Provide variation in your pace and speaking techniques.**

■ 6. CLOSE STRONG

Great speeches demand great endings. It will be the last thing your audience hears from you, so you want it to be memorable. You've spent hours on research and preparation, not to mention practice time. You don't want your speech to end in a weak or indecisive manner. You want your leadership qualities to stand out!

First, let's discuss some general rules about ending your presentation. Then we will review specific ways to close.

1. Signal the end of your talk. This should wake up even the sleepiest member of the audience.

   - I really appreciate your attention this morning. Let me leave you with a couple of thoughts.

   - Before I finish, I'm reminded…

   - Let me conclude my comments by…

2. Keep it short. In a 20- to 25-minute presentation, your ending should be no more than two to three minutes. You're looking to add some sizzle and punch. Don't drone on.

3. Reiterate your central theme. You don't have to hit them over the head, but do remind them of your message and the reason for your presentation. And certainly don't introduce any new topics during your close.

4. Be optimistic. A sure way to kill a good speech is to end pessimistically. Even if it's the darkest days of the bear market or you're discussing layoffs within your organization, you've got to give them hope and encouragement. Especially in tough times, that's what leadership is all about.

5. Use your most forceful language. Now is the time to tell it like it is. Be direct.

Types of Closings

In deciding how to close your presentation, first go back and review your objective. If the objective was simply to inform, then you could conclude your speech with a simple summary of the major talking points. On the other hand, if your objective was to persuade or ask for some action on their part, your close should take on a totally different approach. Keep that in mind as we discuss the different ways to conclude your speech.

Simple Summary: This is probably the simplest of endings to a speech. It involves summarizing your speech's main theme and your specific main points. Perhaps it's not as emotionally satisfying for the speaker and the audience, but it does bring closure to your presentation.

Direct Appeal or Call to Action: Here, you are asking the audience to do something – take some action. It could involve a myriad of issues: raise money, change behavior, change their opinion, etc. It typically would call for a stronger and more emotional close.

Inspirational: With this type of close, you're looking to create a certain feeling with your audience – towards you or a certain situation. In this case a touching anecdote, poem or quotation might work well.

Specific Ideas for Closing

Refer back to the beginning: How did you open your presentation – a story, quotation or dramatic statement? Simply remind your audience of your opening comments and add some additional supporting remarks or observations.

Shared Vision: What is your vision for your company, branch, department or the specific situation you're speaking about? If we all do the right thing, how will it turn out? I've often concluded a speech to my sales force by referring to a vision for the future. "A vision where we have the respect of our clients and each other. A vision where each of us has the ability to grow and prosper. A vision where we are feared by our competitors."

Quotes or Anecdotes: With careful selection, these are always a great way to conclude.

• Let me conclude my comments this evening by sharing with you a story about when my son was playing Little League. He was about eight or nine at the time. I showed up late for the game and asked him what the score was. He said, "Dad, we're losing 13-0." I said, "Mike, you don't seem to be upset by that score." He said, "Dad, why should I be upset? We haven't got up to bat yet." Let me tell you that we haven't got up to bat either...

• As I finish my talk to you, let me tell you a story about a young man who went to have his fortune told. As the gypsy read the crystal ball she said, "You will be poor and unhappy until you're 40 years old." He asked, "What happens after that?" Her reply, "After that, you will get used to it." Ladies and gentlemen, the problem we're facing is not something we want to get used to...

• We are all faced with a series of opportunities brilliantly disguised as impossible situations.
    – *Chuck Swindoll*

Appeal to some emotion: What are the strongest passions we have: love of family, love of country and the way we live, pride in ourselves and perhaps who we work for, competition, church, wealth, security, etc. Clearly, when you make this type of appeal, it will be of a more personal nature. It would probably take the form of a personal or third-person story, quotation or poem. And yes, I believe it is appropriate for a business meeting, although you do want to show good judgment in deciding when and how to use it.

■ 7. PRACTICAL TIPS

Length of Speech

It was Mark Twain who said, "Few sinners are saved after the first 20 minutes." Certainly there will be exceptions to this rule, but try to keep your presentation between 20 and 25 minutes in length. You should certainly be able to accomplish your objective within that timeframe. Secondly, unless you're a trained, accomplished speaker, you'll find it difficult to hold the audience's attention for much longer. I'd rather leave the audience wanting more, than run the risk of looking out into the audience and seeing a bunch of people yawning or looking at their watches. Talk about depressing!

Of course, there are times when you are asked to fill a 45- to 50-minute time slot. What do you do? In Granville Toogood's book *The Articulate Executive*, he tells us to "change the medium to break the tedium." Some ideas:

1. Question and answer period (more on that later).
2. Ask an associate or team member to handle part of the presentation.
3. Show a video clip that ties into your presentation.

Here is my suggested breakdown for a 20- to 25-minute presentation:

Introduction: three to four minutes
Body: 15 to 18 minutes
Close: two to three minutes

Write It or Wing It

There are a number of factors which will determine whether you write out your speech and deliver it word-for-word, speak totally on the fly, or do something in between. Clearly, the occasion will be an important consideration. Are you speaking at lunch to a few retail investors or going before the Securities and Exchange Commission? How comfortable and knowledgeable are you with the topic? How skillful are you as a speaker? Have you given the same or similar presentation before?

Here are some thoughts:

1. Although I have never actually read a speech (to me a speech is a conversation), I have written out speeches and then formatted them into an outline. Writing out your presentation is a terrific exercise. It forces you to clarify and organize your thoughts. What's important about your theme and why? What's the best way to express your ideas? How can you convince people that your ideas are valid? What will they object to and why?

   To me, writing out your speech is analogous to preparing a business plan. The plan is important, but what is critical is the process you go through to build the plan – same as a speech. Writing it down makes you think!

   I admit that often I will go to the lectern with a written-out opening and close. They are the most important parts of a speech, and I want my words to be very precise. We'll talk more about stage fright shortly, but if I'm going to have a panic attack, it will happen when I first get up in front of the audience. Even if I don't refer to what I wrote, it's a great comfort to have it there.

   After I've either written out or made a detailed outline of my presentation, I will then transpose that onto five-by-eight-inch index cards (I don't want to squint). The cards will contain the main points of my presentation with key words or phrases for stories I'll tell or points I want to make. Of course, quotes or statistics are written out, although I'll usually have them memorized.

2. If you're using audiovisual equipment, I learned a wonderful technique from my friend and mentor, Joe Plumeri. Joe is an incredible speaker, one of the best. I was amazed how he could speak for 45 to 60 minutes and never refer to a note or piece of paper. Joe's secret, aside from knowing his topic inside and out, was to put his outline or talking points right onto the screen that the audience saw. For example, the audience might see "Marketing Strategy." That would set Joe up for the next four to five minutes. It's a useful and very effective technique.

3. Let me introduce you to the "unspeech" speech. It is the ultimate

in "winging it," yet one that shouldn't frighten most executives.

When I arrived at MFS in 1994, I had my first opportunity to speak to the sales force. Frankly, I didn't want to make a speech. Rather, I wanted to listen to their concerns, ideas and suggestions. I went in front of the group with nothing but a flip chart and a magic marker. I asked them to tell me their concerns, whatever they might be – performance of our products, marketing materials, compensation, dealer relationships, etc. In about five minutes, we had outlined eight to ten topics.

After that, I simply started at the top and asked them how they thought MFS was doing in each category and whether they had any suggestions on how we could improve. Certainly, I shared my views on the topics discussed, but it was mostly the sales force speaking and me listening. It was a great start. I learned what was on their minds, and they came away believing I was a good listener and an advocate for them. Needless to say, this approach can be used in a variety of situations – whether in trying to deal with a special issue, or integrated into a business planning session. You are limited only by your imagination.

Title Your Presentation

A catchy or provocative title can often be used to create interest and turnout for your presentation. This is particularly important in a format where you're part of a series of breakout sessions, and participants must elect which session to attend. Or perhaps you'll be speaking at a branch for financial advisors or at the local Holiday Inn for the investing public. The title of your presentation can encourage interest and attendance. With all the financial information and news in the media, a presentation entitled *Outlook for the Economy* is simply not going to attract many people. Some titles I've used:

- *The Good, the Bad, and the Ugly*
- *Trust Is a Growth Business*
- *What Do We Do Now?*
- *What I Learned During the Last 10,800 Dow Points*

Questions and Answers

Whenever possible, a Q&A session is always a good idea. It allows you to continue to engage the audience on your theme and to receive feedback. It also can create a more intimate and open feeling with the audience. I've seen many average presentations turn into outstanding ones because the speaker demonstrated his knowledge and openness during the Q&A session. Just remember, you're still on. Don't be unprepared or too casual, or you run the risk of losing all the credibility and good will you've worked so hard to establish.

Here is a checklist of ideas:

1. Come prepared. Consider potential questions and answers beforehand. If you're to appear before the media or in another highly visible situation, practice with some of your associates or work with a public relations firm

2. Set up the Q&A session properly. Don't be shy in declaring any ground rules.

   I'm delighted to answer any questions at this time. Just a reminder: I'm not a research analyst, so please, no questions about individual securities.

3. Be prepared for silence when you ask for questions. Once you get that first question, others will follow. After you've asked for questions and no one raises their hand, to elicit the first one, look at the audience and with a big smile say, "OK, I'm not leaving the room until I get at least one question." As an alternative, you could ask yourself a question (a tough one) or consider having one or two planted in the audience.

4. Restate the question to be sure you got it right and the audience heard it. It also gives you time to think about your answer.

5. Be brief. Don't over-answer and go into a lengthy discourse.

6. If you don't know the answer, say so. Better to appear honest and human than to get caught in a false statement. Simply tell the questioner you'll get back to them with the answer.

7. One of the most common challenges in a Q&A session is the person who really doesn't want to ask a question, but wants to make a speech. Please note that this usually annoys the audience as much as the speaker.

   First of all, don't ever forget that this is your program, and you must always be in control of it. At the same time, remember to be courteous to all audience members, or you run the risk of alienating them. With this situation, I'd first jump in and ask the person what their question is. If that fails, I'd simply look at my watch and say, "We are running out of time. We'll have to move on. Any other questions?"

8. In Brent Filson's book *Executive Speeches,* he discusses doing a quick summary at the end of the Q&A. He's right. Just saying, "Thank you" and walking off seems pretty anticlimactic. It is a great opportunity to not only thank people for their attention, but also to take 30 to 45 seconds to restate your main points, or to use highlights from the Q&A to further advance your theme.

Stage Fright

It's a little-known fact, but Winston Churchill, in his second speech to the House of Commons, forgot the lines of his memorized text and fainted. Some nervousness can and does happen to everyone. Understand that a little anxiety is natural and, in fact, can help energize you. It's when it adversely affects your performance (dry mouth, shaky knees and shallow breathing will do that), that you must guard against.

Some ideas to ensure that the butterflies will fly in formation:

• Being well prepared and confident in your presentation is critical. Stage fright comes from "fear of failure" and the body's physiological ready reaction to that. Don't even allow failure to cross your mind. This means practicing your presentation at least two or three times. And I don't mean sitting around going over the presentation in your mind. I mean a full dress rehearsal. That means standing, using the visual aids planned, and speaking out loud! Your notes or written words will seem different when spoken. Trust me, you will make revisions.

- Always arrive early. If your presentation involves sound or video equipment, a stage, a podium, etc., work with the audiovisual technicians to assure that everything is working properly. How many times have you seen a speaker go to the podium and something is amiss? You don't want that to happen to you! Also, and this is important, go onto the stage and make sure you feel comfortable with the set-up. Visualize the audience in their seats and think about your opening comments. Visualize the audience warming up to you and enjoying your presentation. Feel confident that you've prepared well, and are going to enjoy this opportunity to make your presentation and show your leadership. Visualization is a powerful concept. These visuals will carry over to your presentation.

  And by the way, as long as you're at your presentation early, greet, meet and shake hands with some of the audience. Where are they from? What do they do? Just a little bit of that will help you realize that when you go on stage, the audience members are not the enemy, but a group of warm, friendly people.

- Many speakers and performers find it helpful to do breathing and physical exercise before going on stage. Of course, that's easy for an actor, but what about a speaker who is in the audience just before her introduction? A couple of ideas:

  1. Sit upright in your chair and breathe deeply and regularly.

  2. Reach down on both sides and grab the bottom of the chair. Pull up hard and hold for a few seconds. Repeat a few times. Or if you have a table in front of you, put your palms up underneath and push up. What you're doing, quite simply, is releasing some tension.

  3. Unobtrusive yawning or flexing can help relax the face muscles.

P.S. And don't drink ice-cold water or a beverage before or during your presentation. It tightens up the vocal cords.

PART THREE

■

Quotes and Anecdotes

· SUBJECTS ·

ADVERSITY ————————————

Murphy's Law: "If anything can go wrong, it will."
Murphy's Corollary: "If nothing can go wrong, it still will."
Nichol's Observation: "Murphy was an optimist."

Seven times down, eight times up. – JAPANESE PROVERB

Our greatest glory is not in never failing, but in rising up every time we fail. – RALPH WALDO EMERSON

In times like these, it's important to remember there have always been times like these. – PAUL HARVEY

'Tis easy enough to be pleasant, when life flows like a song. But the man worthwhile is the one who will smile when everything goes dead wrong. – ELLA WHEELER WILCOX

The way I see it, if you want the rainbow, you gotta put up with a little rain. – DOLLY PARTON

Show me someone who has done anything worthwhile, and I'll show you someone who has overcome adversity. – LOU HOLTZ

We have no right to ask when a sorrow comes, "Why did this happen to me?" Unless we ask the same question for every joy that comes our way. – PHILIP E. BERNSTEIN

THE ART OF LIVING ————————

I had a lot of troubles in my life, but most of them never happened. – MARK TWAIN

I try to be cynical, but it's so hard to keep up. – LILY TOMLIN

Resentment is like drinking poison and waiting for the other person to die. – CARRIE FISHER

We cannot become what we need to be by remaining what we are.
— MAX DE PREE

Lead us not into temptation. Just tell us where it is, and we'll find it.
— ANONYMOUS

A halo has to fall only a few inches to become a noose.   — ANONYMOUS

You can get further with a kind word and a gun than with just a kind word.
— ALPHONSE CAPONE

Honesty is the best policy, unless you're an extremely good liar.
— ANONYMOUS

Power corrupts, but absolute power is really neat.   — ANONYMOUS

When you find yourself in a hole, stop digging.   — WILLIAM SAFIRE

People are unreasonable, illogical and self-centered.
    Love them anyway.
If you do good, people will accuse you of selfish ulterior motives.
    Do good anyway.
If you are successful, you will win false friends and true enemies.
    Succeed anyway.
Honesty and frankness make you vulnerable.
    Be honest and frank anyway.
The good you do today will be forgotten tomorrow.
    Do good anyway.
The biggest people with the biggest ideas can be shot down by the smallest people with the smallest minds.
    Think big anyway.
People favor underdogs but always follow top dogs.
    Fight for some underdogs anyway.
What you spend years building may be destroyed overnight.
    Build anyway.
Give the world the best you've got and you'll get kicked in the teeth.
    Give the world the best you've got anyway.   — DR. ROBERT SCHULLER

ATTITUDE _____

An optimist is someone who goes after Moby Dick in a rowboat and takes the tartar sauce with him. – ZIG ZIGLAR

I complained because I had no shoes until I met a man who had no feet. – MILDRED LEO

An optimist loans his car to his son. A pessimist doesn't. A cynic did. – ANONYMOUS

Your attitude is your choice. You make it. – DENIS WAITLEY

It may not be your fault for being down, but it's got to be your fault for not getting up. – STEVE DAVIS

Remember: whatever game you play, 90 percent of success is from the shoulders up. – ARNOLD PALMER'S FATHER

What is the difference between an obstacle and an opportunity? Our attitude towards it. Every opportunity has a difficulty and every difficulty has an opportunity. – J. SIDLOW BAXTER

CHANGE _____

In a competitive world you have two possibilities. You can lose, or if you want to win, you can change. – LESTER THUROW

We all see and understand the need for change, and instinctively avoid it at all costs. – WARREN BENNIS

A great wind of change is blowing. That gives you either an imagination or a hell of a headache. – CATHERINE II, PARAPHRASED

The man who never alters his opinion is like standing water, and breeds reptiles of the mind. – WILLIAM BLAKE

To improve is to change; to be perfect is to change often.

– SIR WINSTON CHURCHILL

The future never just happened. It was created.

– WILL DURANT

If we are to perceive all the implications of the new, we must risk, at best temporarily, ambiguity and disorder.

– ANONYMOUS

Panta rei – all is flux – [therefore] you cannot step twice into the same river.

– HERACLITUS

Today, loving change, tumult, even chaos is a prerequisite for survival, let alone success.

– TOM PETERS

Keep constantly in mind how many things you yourself have witnessed change already. The universe is change, life is understanding.

– MARCUS AURELIUS

Keep changing. When you're through changing, you're through.

– BRUCE BARTON

Who desires constant success must change his conduct with the times.

– NICCOLO MACHIAVELLI

Never change a winning game; always change a losing one. – BILL TILDEN

If in the last few years, you haven't discarded a major opinion, or acquired a new one, check your pulse, you may be dead. – GELETT BURGESS

COMMUNICATION ─────────────

Leo's Law of Public Speaking – Nice Guys Finish Fast.

It's important to remember that you should finish speaking before the audience finishes listening.

– ANONYMOUS

[When communicating to a large or mass audience]: I imagine I'm talking to a single person.

– RED BARBER

This report, by its very length, defends itself against the risk of being read.

– SIR WINSTON CHURCHILL

People, including managers, do not live by pie charts alone – or by bar graphs or three-inch statistical appendices to 300-page reports. People live, reason, and are moved by symbols and stories. – TOM PETERS

To communicate, put your thoughts in order, give them a purpose, use them to persuade, to instruct, to discover, to seduce. – WILLIAM SAFIRE

I never give 'em hell. I just tell the truth and they think it's hell.

– HARRY S TRUMAN

Anyone who isn't confused here doesn't really understand what's going on. – NIGEL WRENCH

Even a nod from a person who is esteemed is of more force than a thousand arguments or studied sentences from others. – PLUTARCH

People will accept your idea more readily if you tell them Benjamin Franklin said it first. – COMIN'S LAW

COMPETITION ─────────────────

You can't run with the top dogs if you're going to pee with the puppies.

– ANONYMOUS

The humility to prepare gives me the confidence to perform.

– VINCE SCULLY

Don't be afraid of opposition. Remember, a kite rises against the wind, not with it. – ANONYMOUS

There's no column on the scorecard headed "remarks."

– SIDNEY LANSBURGH, JR.

Winning isn't everything, but wanting to win is. – VINCE LOMBARDI

When you win, nothing hurts.   – JOE NAMATH

Whoever is winning at the moment will always seem to be invincible.
                                                         – GEORGE ORWELL

The thrill, believe me, is as much in the battle as in the victory.
                                                         – DAVID SARNOFF

The breakfast of champions is not cereal, it's the competition.
                                                         – NICK SEITZ

The trouble with the rat race is that even if you win, you're still a rat.
                                                         – LILY TOMLIN

DECISION MAKING

You don't save a pitcher for tomorrow. Tomorrow it may rain.
                                                         – LEO DUROCHER

One day Alice came up to a fork in the road and saw a Cheshire cat in a tree. She asked the cat, "Would you tell me please, which way I ought to walk from here?" The cat's reply: "That depends a good deal on where you want to get to."   – LEWIS CARROLL

One of our ironclad rules is "Never do business with anybody you don't like." If you don't like somebody, there's a reason. Chances are it's because you don't trust him, and you're probably right. I don't care who it is or what guarantees you get – cash in advance or whatever. If you do business with somebody you don't like, sooner or later you'll get screwed.   – HENRY V. QUADRACCI

Impulse manages all affairs badly.   – PORTUGUESE PROVERB

A wise man sometimes changes his mind, but a fool never.
                                                         – ARABIC PROVERB

If you get all the facts, your judgment can be right; if you don't get all the facts, it can't be right.   – BERNARD BARUCH

If you put everything off till you're sure of it, you'll get nothing done.
– NORMAN VINCENT PEALE

Make every decision as if you owned the whole company.
– ROBERT TOWNSEND

ECONOMICS

The only function of economic forecasting is to make astrology look respectable. – ANONYMOUS

Economists are people who work with numbers but don't have the personality to be accountants. – ANONYMOUS

I believe that economists put decimal points in their forecasts to show they have a sense of humor. – WILLIAM SIMON

An economist is an expert who will know tomorrow why the things he predicted yesterday didn't happen today. – LAURENCE J. PETER

To most of us, the leading economic indicator is our bank account.
– JOE MOORE

Waiting for supply-side economics to work is like leaving the landing lights on for Amelia Earhart. – WALTER HELLER

It's a recession when your neighbor loses his job; it's a depression when you lose your own. – HARRY S TRUMAN

An economist is a man who states the obvious in terms of the incomprehensible. – ALFRED KNOPF

An economist is a man who can tell you what can happen under any set of circumstances, and his guess is liable to be as good as anyone else's.
– WILL ROGERS

An economist is a person who sees something work in practice, and wonders if it will work in theory. – RONALD REAGAN

Three economists went out deer hunting, and almost immediately came upon a magnificent 12-point buck. The first economist fired, and missed the buck by a good ten feet to the left. The second economist's shot then went ten feet wide to the right. At that point, the third economist pumped his fist in the air, and yelled, "Got him!"

ETHICS

One man with courage makes a majority. — ANDREW JACKSON

A corporation cannot blush. — ANONYMOUS

The louder he talked of his honor, the faster we counted our spoons. — RALPH WALDO EMERSON

Greed is good. Greed is right. Greed clarifies, cuts through and captures the essence of the evolutionary spirit. Greed – mark my words – will save the USA. — MICHAEL DOUGLAS IN *WALL STREET*

The best way to keep one's word is not to give it. — NAPOLEON BONAPARTE

Nature knows no indecencies, man invents them. — MARK TWAIN

A thing worth having is a thing worth cheating for. — W.C. FIELDS

Goodness consists not in the outward things we do, but in the inward things we are. — EDWIN HUBBLE CHAPIN

Remember: one lie does not cost you one truth, but the truth. — FREDRICK HEBBEL

Trust everybody, but cut the cards. — FINLEY PETER DUNNE

If you tell the truth, you don't have to remember anything. — MARK TWAIN

Always do right. This will gratify some people and astonish the rest. — MARK TWAIN

In matters of conscience, the law of the majority has no place.
– MOHANDAS K. GANDHI

When in doubt, don't.
– SAUL W. GELLERMAN

Temptation is not always invitation.
– OLIVER WENDELL HOLMES

You are not to do evil that good may come of it. [*Non faciat malum ut inde veniat bonum.*]
– LEGAL MAXIM

He that lies down with the dogs will rise up with the fleas.
– BARBER

A 6th grade boy goes to his dad and says, "I heard this word in class but I don't know what it means. What is Ethics?"

"Son," his father says, "you've come to the right person. I'm an attorney and that is a word we use a lot in my profession. Let me give you an example of ethics. Just last week a blind man came into my office for a consultation. When we were done, he asked me what he owes me. I said $200. Well, son he actually handed me three $100 bills. Now listen carefully because here's the ethics part – I'm asking myself, 'Do I tell my partner?'"

FORECASTS

Never make forecasts, especially about the future.
– SAMUEL GOLDWYN

The rule of staying alive as a forecaster is to give 'em a number or give 'em a date, but never give 'em both at once.
– JANE BRYANT QUINN

He who lives by the crystal ball will end up eating ground glass.
– ANONYMOUS

I have but one lamp by which my feet are guided, and that is the lamp of experience. I know of no way of judging of the future but by the past.
– PATRICK HENRY

The only thing we know about the future is that it is going to be different.
– PETER DRUCKER

There are two classes of people who tell us what is going to happen: those who know they don't know and those who don't know they don't know.
– JOHN KENNETH GALBRAITH

It is a mistake to look too far ahead. The chain of destiny can only be grasped one link at a time.
– SIR WINSTON CHURCHILL

GOALS

Ah, but a man's reach should exceed his grasp – or what's a heaven for?
– ROBERT BROWNING

Go as far as you can see, and when you get there, you will see farther.
– ANONYMOUS

Some men see things as they are and say "Why?" I dream things that never were and say "Why not?"
– GEORGE BERNARD SHAW

Not failure, but low aim is a crime.
– JAMES RUSSELL LOWELL

Vision is the art of seeing the invisible.
– JONATHAN SWIFT

The most pathetic person in the world is someone who has sight but has no vision.
– HELEN KELLER

No one regards what is before his feet; we all gaze at the stars.
– QUINTUS ENNIUS

IDEAS

A new idea is delicate. It can be killed by a sneer or yawn, it can be stabbed to death by a quip, and worried to death by a frown on the right man's brow.
– CHARLES BROWER

Man's mind, stretched to a new idea, never goes back to its original dimensions.
– OLIVER WENDELL HOLMES

If at first the idea is absurd, then there is hope for it.

– ALBERT EINSTEIN

One doesn't discover new lands without consenting to lose sight of the shore for a very long time. – ANDRE GIDE

The best way to have a good idea is to have a lot of ideas.

– DR. LINUS PAULING

INVESTING

On long-term track records: There is no such thing as a lucky marathon runner. – MARK FREEMAN

The best golfer is the one who doesn't hit a few great shots, but who hits the fewest bad ones. Same with investing. – ANONYMOUS

It is not the return *on* my investment that I am concerned about, it is the return *of* my investment. – WILL ROGERS

Bulls can make money.
Bears can make money.
Pigs always get slaughtered. – WALL STREET SAYING

Now is always the most difficult time to invest. – BERNARD BARUCH

October. This is one of the particularly dangerous months to speculate in stocks. The others are July, January, September, April, November, May, March, June, December, August and February. – MARK TWAIN

If only God would give me a sign! Like making a large deposit in my name in a Swiss bank. – WOODY ALLEN

I never attempt to make money on the stock market. I buy on the assumption that they could close the market the next day and not re-open it for five years. – WARREN BUFFETT

You should invest in a business that even a fool can run, because a fool will.

– WARREN BUFFETT

To be a successful investor, you don't have to outperform the market; you only have to match it.

– CHARLES SCHWAB

Don't try to buy at the bottom and sell at the top. This can't be done – except by liars.

– BERNARD BARUCH

Investing is really the opposite of gambling. The longer you gamble, the more assured you are of a loss. The longer you invest, the better your assurance that you'll be up.

– MICHAEL MAUBOUSSIN

More money has been lost reaching for yield than at the point of a gun.

– RAYMOND DEVOE, JR.

To paraphrase Leo Durocher: Investing is like church. Many attend. Few understand.

With asset allocation you give up the chance to make a killing so you don't get killed.

– NICK MURRAY

Investing in a market where people believe in efficiency is like playing bridge with someone who has been told it doesn't do any good to look at the cards.

– WARREN BUFFETT

The best thing going for small investors is the stupidity of large investors.

– LOUIS RUKEYSER

Speculative bubbles occur, essentially, when investors are watching what other investors are doing, rather than paying attention to the merits of risk and return.

– PAUL SAMUELSON, JR.

Never invest in any idea you can't illustrate with a crayon.   – PETER LYNCH

Financial genius is a rising stock market.   – JOHN KENNETH GALBRAITH

Time is like the Archimedes lever in investing.   – CHARLES ELLIS

Buying the hot fund is like enlisting in the Japanese Navy the day after Pearl Harbor.
— NICK MURRAY

The key to making money in stocks is not getting scared out of them.
— PETER LYNCH

LEADERSHIP

Leadership is the ability to hide your panic from everyone. — ANONYMOUS

To lead the people, walk behind them. — LAO TZU

Leadership is the capacity to translate vision into reality. — WARREN BENNIS

If you lead the people with correctness, who will dare not to be correct?
— CONFUCIUS

Leadership is practiced not so much in words as in attitude and in actions.
— HAROLD GENEEN

The conductor has the advantage of not seeing the audience.
— ANDRE KOSTELANETZ

When the best leader's work is done the people say, "We did it ourselves."
— LAO TZU

It is best not to swap horses while crossing the river. — ABRAHAM LINCOLN

On the most exalted throne in the world, we are still seated on nothing but our arse. — MICHEL EYQUEM DE MONTAIGNE

The view only changes for the lead dog. — SERGEANT PRESTON OF THE YUKON

The first responsibility of a leader is to define reality. — MAX DE PREE

Neither a wise man nor a brave man lies down on the tracks of history to wait for the train of the future to run over him. — DWIGHT D. EISENHOWER

Boss versus Leader
> The boss drives subordinates; the leader coaches them.
> The boss depends on authority; the leader on good will.
> The boss says, "I"; the leader, "we."
> The boss fixes the blame for the breakdown;
> the leader fixes the breakdown.
> The boss knows how it is done; the leader shows how.
> The boss says, "Go"; the leader says, "Let's go!"   – ANONYMOUS

Speak softly and carry a big stick.   – THEODORE ROOSEVELT

Speak softly and carry a big carrot.   – HOWARD LAUER

Celebrate what you want to see more of.   – TOM PETERS

The most important words in the English language:
> Five most important words: I am proud of you!
> Four most important words: What is your opinion?
> Three most important words: If you please.
> Two most important words: Thank you
> One most important word: You   – ANONYMOUS

Any leader worth following gives credit easily where credit is due. He does not take someone's idea, dress it up and offer it as his own. He offers it as theirs. Otherwise, ideas will soon cease to flow his way. He plays fair with everyone and recognizes the strong points in people as well as the weak ones. He never takes advantage for his own selfish purposes.   – FRANKLIN J. LUNDLING

The first duty of a leader is to make himself be loved without courting love. To be loved without "playing up" to anyone – even to himself.
– ANDRE MALRAUX

Learn to obey before you command.   – SOLON

What you cannot enforce, do not command.   – SOPHOCLES

If you've got them by the balls, their hearts and minds will follow.
– CHARLES COLSON'S LAW

The seven secrets of being a number one boss:
    Develop professional expertise.
    Sharpen your communication skills.
    Cultivate enthusiasm.
    Keep an open mind.
    Pay attention to accomplishments.
    Be accessible.
    Respect your staff (trust your staff as you would your clients).
– CHERYL RESMOUD

Trust men and they will be true to you; treat them greatly and they will show themselves great. – RALPH WALDO EMERSON

If you pick the right people and give them the opportunity to spread their wings and put compensation as a carrier behind it – you almost don't have to manage them. – JACK WELCH

Test fast, fail fast, adjust fast. – TOM PETERS

LISTENING/SILENCE

Silence gives consent. – OLIVER GOLDSMITH

Silence grants the point. – TROUT AND REIS

One often hears the remark, "He talks too much," but when did anyone last hear the criticism, "He listens too much"? – NORMAN AUGUSTINE

Nature has given to men one tongue but two ears, that we may hear from others twice as much as we speak. – EPICTETUS

A closed mouth gathers no feet. – ANONYMOUS

Better to remain silent and be thought a fool than to speak out and remove all doubt. – ABRAHAM LINCOLN

Silence is one of the hardest arguments to refute. – JOSH BILLINGS

It is the province of knowledge to speak, and it is the privilege of wisdom to listen. — OLIVER WENDELL HOLMES

The road to the heart is the ear. — VOLTAIRE

My wife said I never listen to her; at least I think that's what she said. — ANONYMOUS

An open ear is the only believable sign of an open heart. — DAVID AUGSBURGER

I have often regretted my speech, never my silence. — PUBLILIUS SYRUS

There is a story in Arabia which tells of a pupil asking a wise man how he could become a good conversationalist. The sage replied, "Listen, my son." After waiting a while, the pupil said, "I am listening. Please continue your instruction." The sage smiled, "There is no more to tell." — ANONYMOUS

Blessed is the man who, having nothing to say, abstains from giving in words evidence of the fact. — GEORGE ELIOT

He who takes notes listens well. — DANTE'S OBSERVATION

MANAGEMENT

Men are four:
  He who knows not and thinks he knows.
  He is asleep; wake him.
  He who knows not and knows that he knows not.
  He is a fool; shun him.
  He who knows not and doesn't know that he knows not.
  He is a child; teach him.
  He who knows and knows that he knows.
  He is a King; follow him.
                                          — CHINESE PROVERB

If I had to sum up in one word what makes a good manager, I'd say decisiveness. You can use the fanciest computers to gather the numbers, but in the end you have to set a timetable and act. — LEE IACOCCA

Management is getting paid for home runs someone else hits.
— CASEY STENGEL

A man without a smiling face ought not to open a shop.
— CHINESE PROVERB

I praise loudly, I blame softly. — CATHERINE THE GREAT

Pardon all but thyself. — GEORGE HERBERT

Managers can easily become absorbed by form and insufficiently concerned with substance. — PETER LORANGE

The secret of successful managing is to keep the five guys who hate you away from the five guys who haven't made up their mind. — ANONYMOUS

If anything goes bad, I did it. If anything goes semi-good, then we did it. If anything goes real good, then you did it. That's all it takes to get people to win football games. — PAUL "BEAR" BRYANT

Managers are people who do things right, and leaders are people who do the right thing. — WARREN & BURT BENNIS

Great expectations bring great achievements. — ANONYMOUS

Be candid.
I was angry with my friend;
I told my wrath, my wrath did end.
I was angry with my foe;
I told it not, my wrath did grow. — WILLIAM BLAKE

People ask the difference between a leader and a boss. The leader works in the open, and the boss is covert. The leader leads and the boss drives.
— THEODORE ROOSEVELT

Our chief want is someone who will inspire us to be what we know we could be.   – RALPH WALDO EMERSON

Setting an example is not the main means of influencing another, it is the only means.   – ALBERT EINSTEIN

I not only use all the brains I have, but all I can borrow.
                                                      – WOODROW WILSON

If he works for you, you work for him.   – JAPANESE PROVERB

The best executive is the one who has the sense enough to pick good men to do what he wants done and self-restraint enough to keep from meddling with them while they do it.   – THEODORE ROOSEVELT

No "average" man or woman can be a successful manager. Average is a number. A number has:
    No hands to reach out to help.
    No heart to beat faster at the success of someone you have helped.
    No soul to suffer a bit when one of your people suffers.
    An average person lacks the disciplined mind to be tough and the self-confident strength to be gentle.   – WILLIAM MARSTELLER

A good manager is a man who isn't worried about his own career but rather the careers of those who work for him. My advice: don't worry about yourself. Take care of those who work for you and you'll float to greatness on their achievements.   – H.S.M. BURNS

The Lion Tamer School of Management:
Keep them well fed and never let them know that all you've got is a chair and a whip.   – ANONYMOUS

Lead, follow, or get out of the way.   – ANONYMOUS

You can't manage men into battle. You manage things; you lead people.
                                                      – GRACE MURRAY HOPPER

A frightened captain makes a frightened crew.   – LISTER SINCLAIR

It often happens that I wake at night and begin to think about a serious problem and decide I must tell the Pope about it! Then I wake up completely and remember that I am the Pope. — POPE JOHN XXIII

The three most important things you need to measure are customer satisfaction, employee satisfaction and cash flow. — JACK WELCH

Outstanding leaders go out of their way to boost the self-esteem of their personnel. If people believe in themselves, it's amazing what they can accomplish. — SAM WALTON

The first responsibility of a leader is to define reality. The last is to say thank you. In between the leader is a servant. — MAX DE PREE

Consider how hard it is to change yourself and you'll understand what little chance you have of trying to change others. — JACOB M. BRAUDE

Generally speaking, you like to dance with the girl that brung you, and if you can't, sometimes you have to shoot her. — DAVE BONDERMAN

Nothing in the world can take the place of persistence. Talent will not; nothing is more common than unsuccessful men of talent. Genius will not...the world is full of educated derelicts. The slogan "Press on" has solved and always will solve the problems of the human race. — ATTRIBUTED TO CALVIN COOLIDGE

When in charge, ponder; when in trouble, delegate; when in doubt, mumble. — BOREN'S GUIDELINES FOR BUREAUCRATS

What you measure is what you get. — ROBERT S. KAPLAN, DAVID P. NORTON

One's objective should be to get it right, get it out, and get it over. You see, your problem won't improve with age. — WARREN BUFFETT

MARKETING _____

Price is an issue in the absence of value. — THEODORE LEVITT

You don't sell what it is, but what it does. Nobody wants a quarter-inch drill. What they want is a quarter-inch hole.   – THEODORE LEVITT

Would you persuade, speak of interest, not of reason.   – BENJAMIN FRANKLIN

Cutting prices is usually insanity if the competition can go as low as you can.   – MICHAEL PORTER

Create demand.   – CHARLES REVSON

In our factory, we make lipstick. In our advertising, we sell hope.
                                                                         – CHARLES REVSON

Fuel is not sold in a forest, nor fish on a lake.   – CHINESE PROVERB

Kodak sells film, but they don't advertise film. They advertise memories.
                                                                         – THEODORE LEVITT

Benjamin Franklin may have discovered electricity, but it was the man who invented the meter who made the money.   – EARL WILSON

Before you build a better mousetrap, it helps to know if there are any mice out there.   – MORTIMER B. ZUCKERMAN

Listen to the river and you'll catch a trout.   – IRISH PROVERB

Selling and marketing are antithetical rather than synonymous or even complementary. There will always, one can assume, be a need for some selling, but the aim of marketing is to make selling superfluous. The aim of marketing is to know and understand the customer so well that the product or service fits him and sells itself.   – PETER DRUCKER

Those who enter to buy, support me. Those who come to flatter, please me. Those who complain, teach me how I may please others so that more will come. Only those hurt me who are displeased but do not complain. They refuse me permission to correct my errors and thus improve my service.   – MARSHALL FIELD

Most salesmen try to take the horse to water and make him drink. Your job is to make the horse thirsty.
— GABRIEL M. SIEGEL

MONEY

Money follows performance.
— MARIO GABELLI

It doesn't matter if you're rich or poor, as long as you've got money.
— ANONYMOUS

The lack of money is the root of all evil.
— GEORGE BERNARD SHAW

Money, it turned out, was exactly like sex. You thought of nothing else if you didn't have it and thought of other things if you did.
— JAMES BALDWIN

I have enough money to last me the rest of my life, unless I buy something.
— JACKIE MASON

I have enough money to last me the rest of my life, as long as I die by four o'clock.
— HENNY YOUNGMAN

There are three faithful friends: an old wife, an old dog and ready money.
— BENJAMIN FRANKLIN

A fool and his money are soon parted. What I want to know is how they got together in the first place.
— CYRIL FLETCHER

The man who damns money has obtained it dishonorably. The man who respects it has earned it.
— AYN RAND

Money is a good servant, but a bad master.
— HENRY GEORGE BOAN

Money is like manure. If you spread it around, it does a lot of good, but if you pile it up in one place, it stinks like hell.
— CLINT MURCHISON

With money in your pocket, you are wise, and you are handsome, and you sing well, too.
— YIDDISH PROVERB

Money can't buy friends, but you can get a better class of enemy.

– SPIKE MILLIGAN

Money is power, freedom, a cushion, the root of all evil, the sum of all blessings. – CARL SANDBURG

Whoever said money can't buy happiness didn't know where to shop.

– ANONYMOUS

When a fellow says, "It ain't the money, but the principle of the thing," it's the money. – ELBERT HUBBARD

After Clarence Darrow had solved a client's legal problems, the client asked, "How can I ever show my appreciation?"
The lawyer replied, "My good friend, ever since the Phoenicians invented money, there has only been one answer to that question."

If you would have enemies, lend money to your friends.

– CATALONIAN PROVERB

George Raft earned and disposed of about ten million dollars in the course of his career. "Part of the loot went for gambling," he explained, "part for horses, and part for women. The rest I spent foolishly."

When a person with experience meets a person with money, the person with experience will get the money. And the person with the money will get the experience. – ANONYMOUS

When I was young, I thought money was the most important thing in life. Now that I'm old, I know it is. – OSCAR WILDE

To make money, buy some good stock, hold it until it goes up, and then sell it. If it doesn't go up, don't buy it. – WILL ROGERS

Money can't buy happiness, but it will certainly get you a better class of memories. – RONALD REAGAN

MOTIVATION

Motivation will almost always beat mere talent.   – NORMAN AUGUSTINE

The sight of the gallows focuses the mind.   – MIKE PANITCH

Forty thousand wishes won't fill your bucket with fishes.
– FISHERMAN SAYING

Nothing great was ever achieved without enthusiasm.
– RALPH WALDO EMERSON

Confidence Circle: Accomplishment influences confidence, and confidence influences accomplishment.   – HAROLD HOCK

Genius is initiative on fire.   – HOLBROOK JACKSON

If you aren't fired up with enthusiasm, you will be fired with enthusiasm.
– VINCE LOMBARDI

OPENERS

I'm mindful of something a schoolchild wrote on a history test. He wrote "Socrates was a Greek. He lived 2000 years ago. He told people what to do. He was poisoned." So I'm not here to tell you what to do...

When you're a substitute speaker:
Thank you for that warm reception. It's never easy to be a substitute speaker. People look at you the way they look at doing their tax return. They hope for the best, but they're prepared for the worst.

I've been on the road quite a bit lately. My wife gave me a hint that she wasn't happy about it when I said to her this morning, "Goodbye Mother of two." She replied, "Goodbye Father of one."

This is a great opening for a small group or when the turnout is less than expected:

I recently spoke at a meeting where there was only one person in the audience. I figured "Hey, the show must go on," so I did my 30-minute presentation. I finished, and was about to leave, when the guy in the audience got all excited and said, "You can't leave." I asked him why not. He said, "Because I'm the next speaker."

I'll do my best to be brief. However, I can't lay claim to the skill of the Mississippi Baptist Minister who delivered what is reputed to be the shortest sermon on record. It was Sunday in mid-July, the sun was beating down, the air was as thick as grits. The gray-haired man of the cloth stood tall and resolute in front of the suffering congregation. As he wiped sweat from his brow, he glared out at them and declared ominously, "If you think it's hot in here   "

As Mark Twain once said, "Few sinners are saved after the first 20 minutes." I shall be brief.

The Lord's Prayer has 71 words. The Gettysburg Address 271. The Ten Commandments 297. I've been married for 37 years and it only took two words to get to this point. I shall be brief.

How did I come to be here? Well, Bill asked me if I believe in free speech. I said, "Of course." He said, "Great, come on down and give one."

I feel like I did on my wedding night – I'm very warm, and I'm very nervous. But I'm glad to be here.

I shall be so brief that I have already finished.   – SALVADOR DALI

I will be brief with my comments because I learned something about public speaking. You see, for the first ten minutes, you usually have people's attention. For the next ten minutes, some are with you, others are not. However, after 20 minutes, everybody drifts off into sexual fantasies. And I refuse to give you that much pleasure this morning. You know, I used to be upset when I heard that, but then I realized, hey, at least you're enjoying my presentation.

For those, like me, with little hair:

Thanks for that nice introduction. Actually, I needed a little ego boost. You see, last week I went to my barber who charges me $65 for a haircut. I asked him, "Sal, how come you charge me $65 to cut my hair?" He said, "Mr. Leo, I don't charge $65 to cut your hair, I charge $65 to find it."

Today I promise to make you beneficiaries of the single most important lesson I've learned from all the speakers I've heard. I will put it in the form of a blessing, "Blessed is the speaker who keepeth it short and who delayeth not the _____."

Thank you for that very complimentary introduction. It reminds me of the story of the fellow who was introduced as the most gifted business-man in the country, evidenced by the fact that he had made $1 million in California Oil. When he got in front of the audience, he seemed a little embarrassed. He said, "Let me say that it wasn't oil, it was coal. It wasn't California, it was Ohio. It wasn't $1 million, it was $100,000. It wasn't me, it was my brother. And he didn't make money, he lost it. Matters of fact aside, I'm grateful for the kind words."

I'll be brief, because I'm aware of the following facts. The shortest Inaugural address was 135 words, given by George Washington. The longest, given in 1841 by William Henry Harrison, was 9,000 words and two hours long, given in the teeth of a freezing Northeast wind. Harrison came down with a cold and died of pneumonia a month later.

For when you have a tough spot on the program:

I feel like we're in a javelin-throwing contest. I've lost the coin toss, and I'm receiving.

For after lunch or dinner:

In case you didn't notice, this is an all-beef dinner. The milk is from the cows, the meat is from the steer, and now you're going to hear the bull.

Seeing this big crowd reminds me of the time that Winston Churchill was asked if he didn't get impressed with himself because the hall was packed every time he made a speech. Churchill said, "No, every time it starts going to my head, I remind myself that, if instead of making a speech I was being hanged, the crowd would be twice as big."

A new preacher was disappointed to find that only one member of the congregation showed up to hear his sermon. So he asked the parishioner, who was a farmer, "Should I go ahead with my sermon?"

The farmer said, "Well, I don't know about that sort of thing, but I do know this. If I loaded up a truck with hay, took it out to the prairie, and only one cow showed up, I'd feed her."

So the preacher proceeded to deliver a sermon that lasted an hour and a half. When he was done, he asked the farmer, "What did you think?"

"Well, I don't know about that sort of thing, but I do know this," said the farmer. "If I loaded up a truck of hay, took it out to the prairie, and only one cow showed up, I sure wouldn't give her the whole load."

OPPORTUNITY

Wayne Gretzky said play the puck to where it will be. I say get to the ball before your opponent, and get there in a very bad mood. – ANONYMOUS

Two friends are walking by a Catholic Church. One says to the other, "Do me a favor and wait for me. I'm going inside to say my confession."

He gets to the priest and says, "Please forgive me Father, for I have sinned. It's been six months since my last confession. I committed adultery with someone in the Parish."

The priest replies, "My son, this is a very serious offense. You must tell me who you committed this sin with."

"Father, I can't."

"You must. Was it Mrs. O'Grady?"

"Father, I can't."

"Was it Mrs. Marshall?"

"Father, I won't tell."

"If you don't tell, I won't give you absolution. Was it Mrs. Daly?"

"Father, I can't tell you."

The priest demands he leave and ends the confession. When he gets outside, his friend asks him how it went.

"Well, I didn't get absolution, but I got three good leads."

A few years ago, I was late for my son's Little League game. I asked him how they were doing, and he said, "We're losing 13-0." I said, "Mike, you seem to be taking it rather well." He said, "Dad, we haven't got up to bat yet."

The lesson which life repeats and constantly enforces is "look underfoot." You are always nearer the divine and the true sources of your power than you think. The lure of the distant and the difficult is deceptive. The great opportunity is where you are. Do not despise your own place and hour. Every place is under the stars; every place is the center of the world.   – JOHN BURROUGHS

When one door closes, another door opens; but we often look so long and so regretfully upon the closed door, that we do not see the ones which open for us.   – ALEXANDER GRAHAM BELL

If opportunity doesn't knock, build a door.   – MILTON BERLE

If a window of opportunity appears, don't pull down the shade.
                                                        – TOM PETERS

We are all faced with a series of opportunities brilliantly disguised as impossible situations.   – CHUCK SWINDOLL

Don't miss this opportunity. Don't be like me with a girl on my first date at a drive-in movie. She asked me if I wanted to go in the back seat. I told her, "I'd rather stay up front with you."

What is the difference between an obstacle and an opportunity? Our attitude towards it. Every opportunity has a difficulty, and every difficulty has an opportunity.   – J. SIDLOW BAXTER

Yesterday is history. Tomorrow is a mystery. Today is a gift, that's why it's called the present.   – ANONYMOUS

PEOPLE

First-rate people hire first-rate people; second-rate people hire third-rate people.   – LEO ROSTEN

Treat people as if they were what they ought to be and you help them to become what they are capable of being.   – JOHANN WOLFGANG VON GOETHE

Treat employees like partners, and they act like partners.   – FRED ALLEN

He started out at the bottom, and sort of likes it there.
– TENNESSEE ERNIE FORD

PHILOSOPHY OF LIFE

I don't deserve this, but then, I have arthritis and I don't deserve that either.
– JACK BENNY

There are two things to aim at in life: first, to get what you want; and after that, to enjoy it. Only the wisest of mankind achieve the second.
– LOGAN PEARSALL SMITH

You only live once, but if you work it right, once is enough.   – JOE E. LEWIS

Some men go through a forest and see no firewood.   – ENGLISH PROVERB

The difference between a rut and a grave is the depth.   – GERALD BURRILL

The cobra will bite you whether you call it cobra or Mr. Cobra.
– INDIAN PROVERB

The first half of life consists of the capacity to enjoy without the chance; the last half consists of the chance without the capacity.   – MARK TWAIN

A young philosophy student went to the Himalayas to seek wisdom. He came upon a guru and asked, "What is life?"
The guru closed his eyes, thought and said, "Life is the smell of a fresh new rose." "But Master" said the student, "In the Andes, an elderly Inca told me 'Life is a sharp stone.'"
The Himalayan guru replied, "That is *his* life."

Don't smoke too much, drink too much, eat too much or work too much. We're all on the road to the grave, but there's no reason to be in the passing lane. – ROBERT ORBEN

The secret of staying young is to live honestly, eat slowly and lie about your age. – LUCILLE BALL

PLANNING

There is nothing so useless as doing efficiently that which should not be done. – PETER DRUCKER

If our original plan had a lower goal, we would have achieved less. – WILLIAM FOSTER

If we can't figure something out in three weeks, we probably shouldn't bother. – STEVEN GILBERT

The preparation of an annual plan is in itself the end, not the resulting bound volume…To prepare and justify (a plan), people go through a lot of soul-searching analysis and juggling, and it is this mental exercise that is valuable. – ANDREW S. GROVE

The mouse that hath but one hole is quickly taken. – GEORGE HERBERT

He has half the deed done, who has made a beginning. – HORACE

When everything has to be right, something isn't. – STANISLAW LEE

Too swift arrives as tardy as too slow. – WILLIAM SHAKESPEARE

No person can prevent a stupid person from doing the wrong thing in the wrong place at the wrong time – but a good plan should keep a concentration from forming. – CHARLES E. WILSON

Luck sometimes visits a fool, but never sits down with him. – GERMAN PROVERB

It wasn't raining when Noah built the Ark.   – HOWARD RUFF

It isn't the will to win that's important. Everyone has the will to win. What's important is the will to prepare to win.   – BOBBY KNIGHT

SELLING

Everyone lives by selling something.   – ROBERT LOUIS STEVENSON

I am the world's worst salesman; therefore, I must make it easy for people to buy.   – FRANK W. WOOLWORTH

You can close more business in two months by becoming interested in other people than you can in two years by trying to get people interested in you.   – DALE CARNEGIE

People don't care how much you know, until they know how much you care.   – ZIG ZIGLAR

Nothing ever happens until somebody sells something.   – RICHARD M. WHITE

The best way to get everything you need is to help other people get what they need.   – ZIG ZIGLAR

When I believe, I am believed.   – NICK MURRAY

Be everywhere, do everything and never fail to astonish the customer.   – FRANK W. WOOLWORTH

SPEECHES AND SPEAKING

I like the way you always manage to state the obvious with a sense of real discovery.   – GORE VIDAL

The best audience is intelligent, well-educated, and a little drunk.   – ALBEN W. BARKLEY

A speech is a solemn responsibility. The man who makes a bad 30-minute speech to 200 people wastes only a half-hour of his own time. But he wastes 100 hours of the audience's time – more than four days – which should be a hanging offense. – JENKIN LLOYD JONES

I do not object to people looking at their watches when I am speaking. But I strongly object when they start shaking them to make sure they are still going. – LORD WILLIAM NORMAN

Talking and eloquence are not the same thing; to speak and to speak well are two things. A fool may talk, but a wise man speaks. – BEN JOHNSON

Speak clearly, if you speak at all; carve each word before you let it fall. – OLIVER WENDELL HOLMES, JR.

Do not say a little in many words, but a great deal in a few. – PYTHAGORAS

In oratory the greatest art is to hide art. – JONATHAN SWIFT

SUCCESS/WINNING

The secret of success is consistency of purpose. – BENJAMIN DISRAELI

The harder you work, the luckier you get. – GARY PLAYER

The object of war is not to die for your country, but to make the other bastard die for his. – GEORGE S. PATTON

The meek shall inherit the earth, but they'll never increase market share. – WILLIAM MCGOWAN

Show me a good and gracious loser, and I'll show you a failure. – KNUTE ROCKNE

The race may not be to the swift nor the victory to the strong, but that's how you bet. – DAMON RUNYON

Don't wrestle with pigs; you get dirty and they enjoy it.   – ANONYMOUS

I never lost a game. I just ran out of time.   – BOBBY LAYNE

In a negotiation, he who cares less wins.   – ANONYMOUS

I can give you a six-word formula for success: "Think things through – then follow through."   – EDWARD RICKENBACHER

Success: If it is to be, it's up to me.   – ANONYMOUS

It takes 20 years to make an overnight success.   – EDDIE CANTOR

A woman rushed up to famed violinist Fritz Kreisler after a concert and cried, "I'd give my life to play as beautifully as you do."
Kreisler replied, "I did."

We must believe in luck. For how else can we explain the success of those we don't like?   – JEAN COCTEAU

The first rule of winning: Don't beat yourself.   – FOOTBALL ADAGE

Whoever said, "It's not whether you win or lose that counts," probably lost.   – MARTINA NAVRATILOVA

If at first you don't succeed, try, try again, then quit. There's no use being a damn fool about it.   – W.C. FIELDS

I don't know about the key to success, but the key to failure is trying to please everybody.   – BILL COSBY

The toughest thing about success is that you've got to keep on being a success.   – IRVING BERLIN

Failure is never final and success is never ending. Success is a journey, not a destination.   – DR. ROBERT SCHULLER

Success is never final.   – SIR WINSTON CHURCHILL

Wise men learn by other men's mistakes, fools by their own.

– ANONYMOUS

Opportunity is missed by most people because it is dressed in overalls and looks like work.

– THOMAS EDISON

Defeat isn't bitter if you don't swallow it.

– TED ENGSTROM

God is always on the side of big battalions.

– HENRI DE LA TOUR

Always bear in mind that your own resolution to succeed is more important than any one thing.

– ABRAHAM LINCOLN

Success is a trendy word. Don't aim for success if you want it, just do what you love and it will come naturally.

– DAVID FROST

The man who succeeds above his fellow man is the one who early in life discerns his objective, and toward that objective directs all of his powers.

– VINCE LOMBARDI

Declare victory and get out.

– SENATOR GEORGE AIKEN

Eighty percent of success is showing up.

– WOODY ALLEN

TAKING ACTION

A man suffered a severe financial setback. He got on his knees and pleaded, "Dear God, you've got to help me. The only way I can get back on my feet is if I win the lottery. Make me win." Every day he prayed. Weeks went by. With his last breath of hope he cried, "God, please, I beg of you. Let me win the lottery." All of a sudden, a voice came out of the sky: "Give me a break. At least buy a ticket."

Before his 1939 boxing match with Joe Louis, "Two-Ton" Tony Galento summed up his competitive attitude in four words: "I'll moider de bum." Joe Louis knocked him out. We need more than words!

Deliberate with caution, but act with decision and promptness.

– CHARLES CALEB COLTON

Ignorance never settles a question.   – BENJAMIN DISRAELI

In every affair, consider what precedes and what follows, and then undertake it.   – EPICTETUS

There is no more miserable human being than one in whom nothing is habitual but indecision.   – WILLIAM JAMES

Delay is preferable to error.   – THOMAS JEFFERSON

If you put off everything till you're sure of it, you'll get nothing done.

– NORMAN VINCENT PEALE

Politics is the art of postponing decisions until they are no longer relevant.

– HENRI QUEUILLE

Don't hit at all if it is honorably possible to avoid hitting; but never hit soft.

– THEODORE ROOSEVELT

The great end of life is not knowledge but action.   – THOMAS HENRY HUXLEY

Sighted sub. Sank same.   – DAVID FRANCES MILLER, PILOT, U.S. NAVY

Act quickly, think slowly.   – GREEK PROVERB

TAXES _____

There is one difference between a tax collector and a taxidermist – the taxidermist leaves the hide.   – MORTIMER CAPLAN

You don't see me at Vegas or at the races throwing my money around. I've got a government to support.   – BOB HOPE

The U.S. is the only country where it takes more brains to figure your tax than to earn the money to pay it.   – EDWARD GURNEY

There is nothing sinister in so arranging one's affairs as to keep taxes as low as possible. — JUDGE LEARNED HAND

They say there are only two certainties in life, taxes and death. The only difference is, death doesn't get worse every time Congress meets. — SPARK MATSUNAGA

Why does a slight tax increase cost you $200 and a substantial tax cut saves you 30 cents? — PEG BRACKEN

The hardest thing in the world to understand is income tax. — ALBERT EINSTEIN

Almost without exception, forecasts of the effects of taxes on real behavior have exceeded the actual responses. — HENRY J. AARON

Taxpayer – That's someone who works for the Federal Government but doesn't have to take a civil service exam. — RONALD REAGAN

TEAMWORK

Stacey King tells the story of a game during his rookie year with the Chicago Bulls. King scored one point and Michael Jordan scored 69. After the game, a reporter asked King for his reaction to the game. King said, "I'll always remember this as the night that Jordan and I combined to score 70 points."

It's like the beaver told the rabbit as they stared up at the immense Hoover Dam, "No, I didn't actually build it myself, but it was based on an idea of mine."

Top management work is work for a team rather than one man. — PETER DRUCKER

Talent wins games, but teamwork wins championships. — MICHAEL JORDAN

WEALTH _____

He who wishes to be rich in a day will be hanged in a year.

– LEONARDO DA VINCI

I'm opposed to millionaires, but it would be dangerous to offer me the position.
– MARK TWAIN

All heiresses are beautiful.
– JOHN DRYDEN

Don't try to die rich, but live rich.
– THOMAS BIRD

I've been rich and I've been poor; rich is better.
– SOPHIE TUCKER

Bernard Baruch went to his father to tell him he had made his first million. His father did not seem impressed. "I am not even 30 and I already have my first million – and you're not even happy?" Baruch asked. His father replied, "No, my son, I am not impressed. What I want to know is how you will spend it."

Wealth is not his that has it, but his that enjoys it.   – BENJAMIN FRANKLIN

The meek shall inherit the earth – but not the mineral rights.

– J. PAUL GETTY

Wealth isn't primarily determined by investment performance, but by investor behavior.
– NICK MURRAY

WISDOM _____

The Delphic Oracle was asked to name the wisest man in Greece, and Socrates received the accolade. On being told this, Socrates said, "Since the gods proclaim me the wisest, I must believe it; but if that is so, then it must be because I alone of all the Greeks know that I know nothing."

Good decisions come from wisdom. Wisdom comes from experience. Experience comes from bad decisions.
– MALCOLM FORBES

Every man is a damn fool for at least five minutes every day; wisdom consists in not exceeding the limit. – ELBERT HUBBARD

Wisdom is the reward you get for a lifetime of listening when you'd have preferred to talk. – DOUG LARSON

The only fool bigger than the person who knows it all is the person who argues with him. – ANONYMOUS

· APPENDIX ·

Sources for further study and reference

PUBLIC SPEAKING

The Lost Art of the Great Speech by Richard Dowis, AMACOM

The Articulate Executive by Granville N. Toogood, McGraw-Hill Inc.

Executive Speeches by Brent Filson, John Wiley & Sons, Inc.

The Sir Winston Method by James C. Humes, William Morrow & Company, Inc.

Public Speaking by John H. Powers, Wadsworth Publishing Company

The Eloquent Executive by William Parkhurst, Avon Books

Executive's Portfolio of Model Speeches by Dianna Booher, Prentice Hall

Presentations Plus by David A. Peoples, John Wiley & Sons

Salespeak by Terri Sjodin, Summit Publishing Group

Seminars, the Emotional Dynamic by Frank Maselli, Creative Image

ANECDOTES AND QUOTATIONS

The Ultimate Book of Business Quotations by Stuart Crainer, AMACOM

Quotable Business by Louis E. Boone, Random House

Words of Wisdom by William Safire and Leonard Safire, Simon & Schuster

The Wiley Book of Business Quotations by Henry Ehrlich, John Wiley & Sons

The Speaker's Sourcebook I & II by Glenn Van Ekeren, Prentice Hall

The Little Book of Business Wisdom by Peter Krass, Editor, John Wiley & Sons, Inc.

The Manager's Book of Quotations by Lewis D. Eigen and Jonathan P. Siegel, AMACOM

Unwritten Laws by Hugh Rawson, Crown Publishers

The Little Brown Book of Anecdotes by Clifton Fadiman, Editor, Little Brown & Co.

· ABOUT THE AUTHOR ·

Robert A. Leo retired as Vice Chairman of MFS Fund Distributors, Inc. on December 31, 2003. He joined MFS in 1994 from Smith Barney Shearson, where he served as Executive Vice President and Director of Mutual Funds. From 1984 to 1989, Bob was Director of National Sales for Shearson. Prior to 1984, he spent eight years as a Branch Manager and six years as a Financial Consultant, both in Shearson's Dayton, Ohio office.

Bob was Co-Chairman of the Securities Industry Association's Sales and Marketing Committee in 1989, and served as Chair of the Investment Company Institute's Sales Force Marketing Committee for three years. He sits on the Executive Committee and is one of the founders of the Forum for Investor Advice.

Bob is a graduate of the University of Virginia. He lives in New York City with his wife Dorothy. He is delighted that his two children, their spouses and his four grandchildren also live in New York City.